$19.95

The Irish Americans

BRENDA HAUGEN

WE CAME TO AMERICA

MASON CREST PUBLISHERS • PHILADELPHIA

A group of Irish dancers perform during the 2000 St. Patrick's Day parade in Chicago. Americans of Irish descent make up one of the largest population segments in both the United States and Canada. Many Irish Americans have tried to hold onto traditional dance, music, and other aspects of their culture.

The Irish Americans

BRENDA HAUGEN

WE CAME TO AMERICA

MASON CREST PUBLISHERS • PHILADELPHIA

Mason Crest Publishers
370 Reed Road
Broomall PA 19008
www.masoncrest.com

First printing

1 3 5 7 9 8 6 4 2

Library of Congress Cataloging-in-Publication Data
on file at the Library of Congress

ISBN 1-59084-101-8

Table of Contents

WE CAME TO AMERICA

America's Ethnic Heritage

Barry Moreno, librarian

Statue of Liberty/

Ellis Island National Monument

Ethnic diversity is one of the most striking characteristics of the American identity. In the United States the Bureau of the Census officially recognizes 122 different ethnic groups. North America's population had grown by leaps and bounds, starting with the American Indian tribes and nations—the continent's original people—and increasing with the arrival of the European colonial migrants who came to these shores during the 16th and 17th centuries. Since then, millions of immigrants have come to America from every corner of the world.

But the passage of generations and the great distance of America from the "Old World"—Europe, Africa, and Asia—has in some cases separated immigrant peoples from their roots. The struggle to succeed in America made it easy to forget past traditions. Further, the American spirit of freedom, individualism, and equality gave Americans a perspective quite different from the view of life shared by residents of the Old World.

Immigrants of the 19th and 20th centuries recognized this at once. Many tried to "Americanize" themselves by tossing away their peasant clothes and dressing American-style even before reaching their new homes in the cities or the countryside of America. It was not so easy to become part of America's culture, however. For many immigrants, learning English was quite a hurdle. In fact, most older immigrants clung to the old ways, preferring to speak their native languages and follow their familiar customs and traditions. This was easy to do when ethnic neighborhoods abounded in large North American cities like New York, Montreal, Philadelphia, Chicago, Toronto, Boston, Cleveland, St. Louis, New Orleans and San Francisco. In rural areas, farm families—many of them Scandinavian, German, or Czech—established their own tightly knit communities. Thus foreign languages and dialects, religious beliefs, Old World customs, and certain class distinctions flourished.

The most striking changes occurred among the children of immigrants, whose hopes and dreams were different from those of their parents. They began breaking away from the Old World customs, perhaps as a reaction to the embarrassment of being labeled "foreigner." They badly wanted to be Americans, and assimilated more easily than their parents and grandparents. They learned to speak English without a foreign accent, to dress and act like other Americans. The assimilation of the children of immigrants was encouraged by social contact—games, schools, jobs, and military service—which further broke down the barriers between immigrant groups and hastened the process of Americanization. Along the way, many family traditions were lost or abandoned.

Today, the pride that Americans have in their ethnic roots is one of the abiding strengths of both the United States and Canada. It shows that the theory which called America a "melting pot" of the world's people was never really true. The thought that a single "American" would emerge from the combination of these peoples has never happened, for Americans have grown more reluctant than ever before to forget the struggles of their ethnic forefathers. The growth of cultural studies and genealogical research indicates that Americans are anxious not to entirely lose this identity, whether it is English, French, Chinese, African, Mexican, or some other group. There is an interest in tracing back the family line as far as records or memory will take them. In a sense, this has made Americans a divided people; proud to be Americans, but proud also of their ethnic roots.

As a result, many Americans have welcomed a new identity, that of the hyphenated American. This unique description has grown in usage over the years and continues to grow as more Americans recognize the importance of family heritage. In the end, this is an appreciation of America's great cultural heritage and its richness of its variety.

1 Famine

In the 1840s, Ireland was one of the poorest countries in Europe. Most of the people lived on small farms and depended on the potato crop for their everyday existence. Potatoes don't require expensive or complicated tools to plant or tend them. The seedlings are planted in rows and covered with dirt. Once the seedlings were planted, farmers could work at other jobs to make money. Many traveled to nearby England for jobs as laborers or worked in shipyards. The farmers knew they could be back home in time to harvest their own crops. The potatoes could then be stored and eaten all year, until the next crop was ready.

An Irish potato farmer gathers his crop. Potatoes are planted and harvested in Ireland today in much the same way they were 150 years ago. However, the near-total reliance of the Irish people on the potato as a source of nutrition during the mid-19th century turned into a disaster when the potato crop failed for several years during the 1840s. Millions died of starvation; millions more left Ireland to seek new lives in North America.

Normally, a person who eats only one type of food all the time will eventually get sick, because that person does not get all the important nutrients he or she needs. However, potatoes are a great source of vitamins and other important nutrients a person's body needs to stay healthy, so the Irish were able to live almost exclusively off this crop.

Being so dependent on potatoes, however, had some drawbacks. Farmers saved some seedlings to plant the next spring, but the potatoes the families relied upon for their survival didn't keep forever. They had to be eaten by the time the next crop was planted or the potatoes would rot. The summer months were particularly hard for Irish

Stone walls like these separate farm fields throughout Ireland. Many of the walls were built during the famine years. The government of Great Britain, which ruled Ireland at this time, fed the starving Irish in exchange for their work on projects such as building fences, roads, and other structures.

THE FAILED POTATO CROPS

In 1845, a fungus, or blight, hit Ireland's potato fields. While some fields were spared that year, this wasn't the case the following year. The fungus spread easily from one place to another, and no one immediately recognized the danger it posed. The crop failure was nearly total in 1846.

Because so many people depended upon the potato crop for their survival, the situation was immediately serious. Families who existed only by eating potatoes tried to make the rotten crops edible. They grated the rotten potatoes, boiled them, then squeezed them in a cloth or made them into potato cakes. The results were sickness and suffering.

The crop rebounded a bit in 1847, but the small harvest was only enough to feed about one-fifth of the country's population. The crop failed repeatedly through the end of the decade.

The suffering the people endured was particularly hard to take because of the bounty of other food the country's farms were producing. Oats, wheat, barley, and livestock raised in Ireland continued to be exported out of the country by its rulers in Great Britain. A British historian and journalist made a list of the food shipped out of Cork, Ireland, on November 18, 1848—a single day. The list included 300 bags of flour, 300 head of cattle, 239 sheep, 147 bales of bacon, 120 casks and 135 barrels of pork, 542 boxes of eggs, and five casks of ham.

Immigrants would later tell their children tales of the food convoys which, under armed guard, marched past starving men, women, and children whose mouths were green from eating grass.

AN IRISH EPITAPH.

This British cartoon pokes fun at the Irish and the affection they held for their country. Although most of the emigrants from Ireland hoped to return one day, few were able to do so.

families as they waited for the potato harvest. A report on the poor in Ireland in 1837 said that more than two million families were nearly starving every summer.

In 1845, things got worse. A disease attacked the potato crops, and the potatoes began to rot in the fields. Stories were being told everywhere about the horror Irish people felt at finding their potatoes rotting in the fields, turning black and mushy. One Irish writer of the time told a story about a man who found that his potatoes had been hit by the **blight**. "[He] went out to the garden for potatoes for a meal. He stuck his spade in the pit, and the spade was swallowed. The potatoes had turned to mud inside. He shrieked and shrieked. The whole town came out."

Had the problem with diseased potatoes only lasted for one year, it's unlikely many Irish people would have left their homeland. Throughout history, Irish people have been known for the love they hold in their hearts for their native land. But the crop failures continued through the 1840s. They were followed by other diseases that killed many of the starving Irish peasants. Soon, more than a million people were dead from the potato famine. For a few years, the government of Great Britain, which controlled Ireland at the time, provided food and other assistance. By 1848, however, the relief efforts had mostly ended. Many people decided leaving Ireland and moving to another country was their only chance for survival. One of the many millions of immigrants who left Ireland during this time was a man named Henry Johnson.

The Journey Begins

When Henry Johnson boarded a ship in Ireland that was bound for New York City, he left with hope for the future. But he was sad as well, because he knew he'd be separated from his wife and children, at least for a time. He planned to get settled in the United States and find a job. Then he could afford to send money to his family, so they too could leave Ireland and join him in America.

By the middle of the 19th century, more than 8 million people lived in Ireland—most in complete poverty. Because of the famine, about a million people said farewell to the island's green shores.

But Henry and the others from Ireland who *emigrated* to the New World during the famine years were not the first to make the journey across the Atlantic Ocean. Among the earliest Irish to travel abroad were religious *missionaries* who ventured out on a voluntary basis. One of the most famous of these was Brendan the Navigator, an Irish monk. According to Irish legend, in the seventh century Brendan sailed west across the Atlantic Ocean and found land. In addition, an Irish sailor from Galway was an important member of Christopher Columbus's crew during his 1492 voyage to the New World. However, historians diagree on this Irishman's name.

The Irish also played a key role in the American colonies, starting many communities and helping to form the backbone of what was to become the United States of America. It's estimated that about 100,000 Irish came to the colonies, mainly between 1717 and 1770. Many also made their mark in the colonies' fight for independence from British rule. Irish immigrants and Irish Americans are said to have accounted for between one-third and one-half of the American Revolutionary War forces, including nearly 1,500 officers and 26 generals. In fact, George Washington chose Commodore John Barry, an Irishman, to create, and later command, the first U.S. Navy.

Those who came to the United States and Canada in the 19th century were mainly immigrants forced to leave their homeland because of economic and political reasons. From 1825 to 1845, more than 800,000 Irish immigrants came to North America. In the late 1820s and the beginning of the 1830s, about two-thirds of those people moved to Canada, mainly settling in Nova Scotia, Newfoundland, and New Brunswick. Others ventured further, following the St. Lawrence River in to Quebec, Ontario, and other parts of the country.

In Canada, many Irishmen found happiness and prosperity, including one farmer who said, "I may say I never wrote anything of this country but the truth and I am sorry at nothing so much as that I did not come sooner to it."

Irish emigration patterns began to change in the mid 1830s, when more chose the United States as their destination. From that time on,

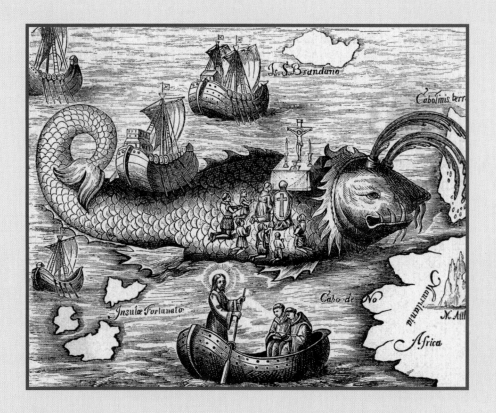

This drawing depicts a legendary story about St. Brendan, a sixth-century Irish monk who sailed a small coracle—a boat made of animal skin stretched over a wooden frame—out into the Atlantic Ocean. Brendan, sometimes called "the Bold" or "the Navigator," intended to spread Christianity to new lands. According to the legend, when Brendan landed on one island, he built an altar and held mass. Afterward, Brendan and the other monks realized that the island was in fact a whale. Brendan may have landed in North America several hundred years before the Vikings, and nearly 1,000 years before Christopher Columbus.

Liverpool, shown in this 19th-century painting, was an important port on England's west coast. It was the main point of departure for thousands of Irish immigrants to the New World.

America would become home to three out of every five Irish searching for new places to call home. New York received more than half the Irish who came to America. Nearly 652,000 immigrants from Ireland arrived on 2,743 voyages during the famine years, according to U.S. immigration records. Boston, Baltimore, and Philadelphia also were the destinations of many of the immigrant ships.

The cost of passage varied. Trips to Canada cost as little as $11. The cheapest fares to New York were around $17.50.

By far, the greatest number of Irish people to leave their homeland in recorded history were those who emigrated during the potato famine of 1846 to 1850. Before this terrible tragedy, the population of Ireland stood at about eight million, two-thirds of whom depended upon farming for their livelihood. During the famine years, about one million starved to death and another 1.5 million moved to other countries, such as the United States and Canada. Henry Johnson was among that number.

As was the case with most of the Irish immigrants during the famine years, Henry Johnson found passage to the United States aboard a boat that departed from Liverpool, England. The majority of those leaving Ireland took ferries across the Irish Sea to Liverpool, where bigger ships would take them across the ocean. Thousands of ships crossed the Atlantic carrying Irish emigrants during the famine years.

The trip from Liverpool to North America aboard the ships lasted anywhere from a month to two months or more, depending upon the conditions at sea. Conditions on the ships varied from vessel to vessel as well.

Many of the ships taking emigrants to the New World weren't originally designed to transport people, but the demand for transportation across the ocean led many in the shipping industry to quickly transform their cargo carriers into passenger ships. In a matter of two or three days, a ship could be equipped with bunks made from planks of wood and a few nails. These ships were not very comfortable.

Safety was often an issue. The passengers cooked in makeshift barbecues on the decks of the ships. Though cooking wasn't allowed on days with strong winds, fires still got out of control at times.

Ireland was a country filled with stone ruins by the time people began to emigrate to North America. Today, sites like Blarney castle are popular tourist attractions.

THE FATHER OF THE AMERICAN NAVY

Among the important figures in the Revolutionary War are many Irishmen. Perhaps one of the most famous is Commodore John Barry, who is called the father of the American Navy.

Born in County Wexford, Ireland, in 1745, Barry came to America when he was 15, making Philadelphia his home.

Once a cabin boy, Barry became captain of a schooner when he was 21. By age 29 he was commanding a ship involved in trade across the Atlantic.

At the onset of the Revolutionary War, Barry offered his services to his new country and made history when he captured the first British ship. In fact, he fought and won the first and last naval battles of the war.

When the war was done, Barry returned to the merchant seas, but his country had bigger things in mind for him. The United States had adopted its Constitution, and the country's leaders knew they would have to maintain a strong system of defense if the United States was to remain free. Because of this, the army and navy were formed. George Washington chose Barry to create and later command the first U.S. Navy. He continued to serve his country until his death September 13, 1803.

Disease was a problem, too. Not all of the emigrants were healthy when they made the Atlantic crossing, and diseases easily passed from person to person in the cramped quarters on the ships.

Henry Johnson was among the lucky ones to make it safely to the United States, though his trip was far from uneventful. After an eight-week journey across the Atlantic Ocean, Henry arrived in New York City and wrote a letter to his wife, Mary, September 18, 1848:

I have had a rather tough time of it. I was a week in Liverpool before the ship sailed on July 7th. We started with a fine, fair breeze and got along well until the third day when it came on to blow very hard. I was lying in my berth sleeping when I was awakened with a cry, "Ship's lost, the ship's sinking." I started up, and such a sight! Men, women, and children rushing to the upper deck, some praying and crossing themselves, others with faces as white as a corpse. On deck they were gathered like sheep in a pen, crying on the captain to save them.

I seen sailors rushing down to the lower deck and I followed, determined to know for myself, and there, sure enough, the water was coming in through one of the portholes at the bow as thick as a large barrel. For a long time all the efforts of the sailors and two mates was [unable] to stop it, and they give it up in despair and came and told the captain to lower the boats. He cursed them and told them to try it again, but the first mate refused and told him to go himself, which he did, telling the man at the helm at the same time to put the ship before the wind, a very dangerous experiment at the time, as we were near some rocks on the Irish Coast. However, he went down and got it partially stopped which partly quieted the fears of the passengers, although some of them didn't get over it until the end of the voyage. I took the matter coolly enough. I knew if we were to go down I might as well take it kindly as not, as crying wouldn't help me. Under this impression I enjoyed the scene about me well.

The scene about him sounded like one of chaos and fear. Most of the others on board weren't as outwardly calm as Henry. One of about 40 Protestants on the vessel, Henry's views of the reactions of the 450 Catholics on board may have been a little skewed. According to Henry, as the ship continued to take on water, the Catholics sprinkled holy water, prayed, cried, and crossed themselves before containing their emotions enough to help pump the water from the ship. One could only imagine the range of emotions the passengers felt, first in leaving their beloved homeland for a strange and faraway place and uncertain future, and then finding that their ship was sinking.

Regardless, the captain of this particular ship was able to get the situation under control and continue the voyage successfully.

"We got all right again and went on our right course," Henry said.

Immigrants huddle in blankets on the steerage-class deck of the S.S. *Pennland*, a steam liner headed for New York City. Most of the Irish immigrants who came to the United States and Canada had little money, and could only afford steerage tickets. They made the journey across the Atlantic in cramped, smelly quarters. This photograph was taken in 1893.

3 The Coffin Ships

Many other Irish immigrants were not as lucky as Henry Johnson. Many of the ships carrying immigrants across the Atlantic Ocean weren't fit for human passengers. Anxious to make a quick buck, ship owners hastily converted their cargo ships to accommodate passengers by investing in a few nails and pieces of wood to make bunks.

Greed also led captains to sail when they otherwise wouldn't. Icebergs sank some ships and winter cold caused suffering on others. Late sailings to Canada always were dangerous. In 1849 alone, four ships were known to have gone down after hitting ice. Ports on the St. Lawrence closed as soon as ice built up in the autumn. And as the weather grew colder, the passengers were bound to suffer.

The crowded, unsanitary conditions on the "coffin ships," as they were later called, also were breeding grounds for diseases, which often were brought on board by passengers or members of the ships' crews. Shortages of food and clean water also caused diseases to spread quickly throughout the ships.

According to law, passengers on the ships were supposed to be provided with six pints of water each day. The six pints would be used to drink, cook, and wash. If the trip lasted longer than was planned, everyone on board the ship—including members of the crew—would end up going thirsty once the water **rations** had been exhausted.

Laws also required that each passenger get a total of seven pounds of potatoes, oatmeal, bread, biscuit, rice, or flour each week. That meant the person would have one pound of food each day, just enough to survive. Again, if the trip took longer than expected, **provisions** would run out and everyone would go hungry.

Throughout the famine years, Passengers' Acts were passed and refined by the American and British governments to help make conditions on the ships better for the emigrants, but the two governments' laws didn't always match. For instance, Britain allowed the ships to carry more passengers than American law allowed. And with all the ships making the trip and few officials to enforce the laws, the Passengers' Acts often were ignored.

While the emigrants were supposed to have livable conditions while making their journey, even the meager provisions they were given often were not fit for people to eat. Henry Johnson found this to be the case on his ship. He wrote to his wife:

"Up to this time I had not opened my provision box as it was lowered into the hold, but when I did get at it I found the ham alive with maggots and was obliged to throw it overboard. The remainder of the stuff I eat as sparingly of as possible but could not spin them out longer than four weeks, at the end of which time I was obliged to subsist on the ship's allowance which was two pounds of meal or flour and five pounds of biscuit in the week. The pigs wouldn't eat the biscuit so that for the remainder of the passage I got a right good starving."

A BURIAL AT SEA

In his letters home, Henry Johnson described what happened when a man on his deck died just before a storm:

> One poor family in the next berth to me whose father had been ill all the time died the first night of the storm and was laid outside his berth.
>
> The ship began to roll and pitch dreadfully. After a while the boxes, barrels, etc. began to roll from one side to the other, the men at the helm were thrown from the wheel and the ship became almost unmanageable. At this time, I was pitched right into the corpse, and there, corpse, boxes, barrel, women, and children, all in one mess, were knocked from side to side for about 15 minutes. Shortly after, the ship got righted and the captain came down. We sewed the body up, took it on deck, and amid the raging of the storm, he read the funeral service for the dead and pitched him overboard.

While passengers could bring some supplies of their own, many did not have anything to bring, and the small space they were allowed on the ships didn't give them much room to carry anything extra. The immigrants went from struggling to survive in Ireland to struggling to survive on the ships, which caused many of the passengers to concern

This 1870 illustration shows steerage passengers in their crowded sleeping quarters. These primitive conditions became breeding grounds for disease, and many emigrants did not survive the Atlantic crossing.

themselves only with their own survival and that of their families.

1847 ranks as one of the worst years on the famine ships. Of the 100,000 Irish emigrants who headed to North America from Great Britain that year, around 17,000 died at sea and another 20,000 died of disease shortly after reaching their destinations.

At the *quarantine* station at Grosse Isle, Canada, in less than six months in 1847, 8,691 people were admitted to the hospital. The hospital was equipped to handle 200. Nearly 3,500 died.

The hospital staff was not *immune* either. During the famine years, 44 staff members at Grosse Isle died, including 22 nurses and

A LONELY, STORMY PASSAGE

Henry Johnson wrote of his 1848 journey across the Atlantic Ocean, "There was not a soul on board I knew of I might have got a little assistance from, but it was every man for himself. Altogether, it was nearly eight weeks from the time we started from Liverpool until we got to New York, the longest passage the captain said ever he had. Six days before we got in, a regular storm came on with the wind in our favor, and anything I had read or imagined of a storm at sea was nothing to this. We had some very hard gales before, but this surpassed anything I ever thought of. Although there was some danger yet the wind being with us and going at the rate of 13 miles an hour through mountains at sea, I enjoyed it well. In the six days the storm lasted, we made more than we had done for six weeks before. This was the pleasantest time I had though not for some others."

orderlies, four doctors, four Catholic priests, two Protestant clergymen, three policemen, three stewards, and six others who carted away the dead, dug graves, and carried supplies.

The situation wasn't much different in the United States. The Rest Haven Cemetery contains the graves of more than 850 Irish immigrants who died in a quarantine station set up by Boston city leaders. The station was established in June 1847 when fear of *typhus* and *cholera* outbreaks motivated these leaders to check the Irish ships docking in Boston Harbor.

But passing the physical at the Deer Island immigration station in Boston didn't guarantee the health of the immigrants. They often became sick after living in the poor conditions found in the city's Irish ghettos. Without any money, the new arrivals usually were homeless and ended up sleeping along Boston's waterfront area or in doorways with their families.

Irish immigrants to Canada disembark their schooner at Grosse Isle, on the St. Lawrence River. During the famine years, U.S. immigration officials, fearful that a tide of Irish immigrants might engulf them, insisted that some ships be diverted to Canada. By the spring of 1847, the St. Lawrence River was jammed with vessels loaded with Irish immigrants waiting to be processed at the Grosse Isle quarantine station.

4 Arrival

Once Henry Johnson arrived in New York, he searched for a job, but this was no easy task.

Many of the Irish who made the journey to the United States and Canada had been farmers in their homeland, so one might expect them to have the same occupation in their adopted countries. However, that generally wasn't the case.

Farming in the New World was different from what the Irish were accustomed to. Farms were larger—and lonelier. The Irish were used to being close to their neighbors, but in the New World, farm homes could be miles apart.

This Jacob Riis photograph shows immigrant children standing with barrels in an alley crisscrossed with clotheslines at the Gotham Court tenement, New York City. The photo was used by Riis in his book *How the Other Half Lives*, which discussed the problem of urban poverty, especially among immigrants to the United States.

It also was hard for them to get into farming. They had to have money in order to buy land and the necessary tools. However, they wouldn't have any money coming in until the first crops were harvested. What would they eat until that time? Many of the Irish immigrants came across the Atlantic with nothing, so setting up a farm wasn't an option for them.

Some adventurous Irishmen braved the wilderness and took "green-wood farms," areas of land covered with trees. First choosing the best spot to build their homes, they erected small log cabins and then took to clearing the trees one by one. To secure funds for provisions, the settler also would have to work for nearby farmers in order to make some money.

The trees that were cut down were used to keep the cabin warm in the cold months. The ashes were used as ***fertilizer*** for the potatoes the farmer would likely plant once a large enough patch was cleared. The next year, farmers often planted wheat as well.

The work was hard, but that was nothing new for the Irish. The reward was their freedom and their survival, which made up for their toils.

Nova Scotia attracted immigrants with its farmland, but the Irish found the soil to be different from what they were used to in Ireland. As a result, the majority ended up gravitating toward the larger cities.

Prince Edward Island and Newfoundland proved to be the most similar to the immigrants' Irish homeland, and many were drawn to these lands. The soil was ideal for growing potatoes, and the coastlines provided fishing similar to the Irish coastline. Even today, Prince Edward Island and Newfoundland produce more potatoes than any of the other provinces in Canada.

Irish emigrants were attracted to Canadian provinces such as Prince Edward Island and Newfoundland. These cooler areas to the north of the United States had climates that were similar to that of Ireland.

Many Irish also settled in New Brunswick. St. John, New Brunswick, was one of the main ports where immigrants to the New World landed. Starting around 1815, Irish immigrants, many of whom were tradesmen, came to St. John, forming the backbone of that community's workforce. Between 1845 and 1854, more than 30,000 Irish stopped first in St. John. Some stayed, but others

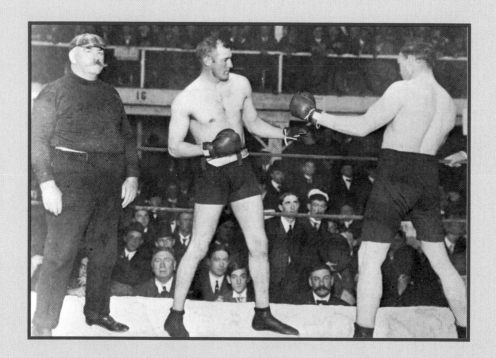

THE CHALLENGER

John L. Sullivan (center) was always looking for a fight.

Born in Boston in 1858 to immigrant parents, Sullivan arguably set the stage for boxing to become the popular sport it is today.

"My name is John L. Sullivan and I can lick any man in the house!" he'd say as he traveled around the country challenging anyone brave enough to take him on for four rounds.

At 17, he weighed 200 pounds and had already had his share of fights with his schoolmates. At 20, he had his first exhibition bout, which he easily won. Soon he was fighting for prize money.

Prizefighting was illegal in most states in 1880. Sullivan and his Irish-American manager, Billy Madden, are credited with breaking down the barriers for boxing as a sport.

Sullivan became a celebrity across the country, continuing to fight well into his 40s.

moved on to the United States, in particular, Boston.

Many of the immigrants who came to the United States stayed in the cities, particularly on the East Coast. Having nothing but each other, the Irish tended to stay together in the **ghettos** of New York, Philadelphia, New Orleans, and Boston. Many of those originally bound for Canada also found their way to these cities.

The hard life these folks had endured in Ireland wasn't made

A large percentage of the Irish people who came to America during the 19th century followed the Roman Catholic faith. In the United States and Canada, this made them a minority. The Irish immigrants sometimes faced discrimination because of their religious beliefs. The immigrants

built churches in their neighborhoods, and opened parochial schools where their children would be taught Catholic beliefs as well as regular school subjects. Many Irish Americans today are Catholic, as are most of the people living in Ireland. This is St. Patrick's Cathedral in Dublin, Ireland.

Once Irish immigrants arrived in the United States, they looked for work. Many worked in construction jobs. Irish laborers dug canals and built railroads. This photograph shows Irish workers laying down track on the Central Pacific Railroad in 1869. In April of that year, a hand-picked team of Irish railroad workers set a record by laying more than 10 miles of track in a day.

much better by the journey. Many were welcomed by thieves and pickpockets, ruthless boarding house operators, and other tricksters hoping to take advantage of the newcomers.

Poor and sickly, few had any education or experience in any profession. They took whatever jobs they could find, which usually ended up being the lowest paying—and most difficult and dangerous—work.

The first generation of Irish famine immigrants worked in a variety of jobs. Some became servants. Others helped to build the railroads throughout the United States and Canada. Still others swept streets, dug canals, cleaned fish, built roads, and tended horse stables.

They also faced **discrimination**. The desperate situation of the Irish immigrants led them to work at just about any job for little pay. This was seen as a threat to Americans already in the workforce. They feared the Irish might take their jobs because they would work for less money. This fear made NINA (No Irish Need Apply) signs commonplace.

Henry Johnson was among those unable to find work. Because of this, he decided to go north to Hamilton, Canada. The Johnson family planned to join him in the United States when Mary and the children could make the Atlantic crossing, but it wasn't to be. Like many of his fellow Irishmen, Henry eventually died of cholera in New York, while Mary and the Johnson children boarded the ship *Riverdale* and sailed for Quebec. ✳

Members of the Emerald Society, a group of Irish Americans within the New York City Police Department, march up Fifth Avenue during a recent St. Patrick's Day parade. Like other immigrant groups, Irish Americans established social groups in the United States and Canada with the goal of helping other immigrants from their homeland succeed.

5. Turning the Corner

Though the first generation of Irish immigrants faced great hardships—poverty, disease, and discrimination—it didn't take long for their fortunes to turn.

In 1855, immigrants to the United States were formally processed at Castle Garden, New York. Here they were warned to watch out for those who would take advantage of them. The immigrants also could get advice about where to stay and how to find a job.

On the other end of the immigrants' trips, officials in Liverpool also were warning passengers of the tricksters they might come across. One brochure given to the emigrants explained:

> As may be supposed, there are many people engaged in the business of forwarding emigrants, and the individuals and companies thus engaged employ a host of clerks or servants (called runners) who try to meet the newcomers on board the ship that brings him or immediately after he has put foot on shore, for the purpose of carrying him to the forwarding offices for which they act. The tricks resorted to in order to forestall a competitor and secure the emigrant would be amusing, if they were not at the cost of the inexperienced and unsuspecting stranger. It is but too true that an enormous sum of money is annually lost to the emigrants by the wiles and false statements of the emigrant runners, many of them originally from their own country and speaking their native language.

Job prospects improved as well. In 1850, about one in 10 of the doctors in Boston had been born in Ireland. By 1880, more than half the Irish born in Boston ranked among the relatively privileged. Joining their ranks was Boston boxer John L. Sullivan, one of the most famous athletes of his time. Not only is Sullivan credited with leading boxing to become the popular sport it is today, he served as a hero for his Irish countrymen.

Andrew Greenlees, a typical immigrant, found work in Plattsburg, New York, as a blacksmith and metal worker. After a time, he grew to feel comfortable in his new homeland. He told his family in the 1850s:

> The customs of this country are quite different. The old and strangers coming here think it quite odd until they get civilised and know how to take right hold to any piece of work and do it up in Yankee fashion, then they get along well and feel quite at home. As respects my health, it never was better, and my trade, I am getting master of it quite fast and I am very comfortably fixed in other respects. I don't have so long hours to work as on a farm: we commence in the morning at half-past-six. As for quitting, we can't be regular, if we have a heavy smelt, we're later and a light smelt, half-past-five. The furnace I'm in runs all year, not as good a chance to make money, but the wages are $1 a day.

During the last decades of the 19th century, the sons of the Irish famine immigrants became plumbers, carpenters, firemen, and policemen. A new wave of immigrants was arriving from Italy and eastern Europe, and these people took the lower-paying jobs. By 1900, Irish-American men made up about 8 percent of the male labor force,

Some Irish Americans became successful as soldiers. The famed Civil War photographer Matthew Brady took this studio portrait of Brigadier General Thomas Francis Meagher, commander of a unit made up of Irish-American troops and called the Irish Brigade. After the Civil War, Meagher served as temporary governor of the Montana Territory until his death in 1867.

A CANADIAN LEGEND

Born in Carlingford, Ireland, in 1825, Thomas D'Arcy McGee is known as one of the fathers of the Canadian Confederation.

McGee was among those fleeing the effects of the famine. Just 17 when he headed for North America, he found his way to the United States. He worked in the newspaper industry, eventually becoming editor of the *Boston Herald*.

Several years later, McGee ended up in Montreal, where he started his own newspaper, *The New Era*. Not afraid to speak his mind, he called for the federation of the British North American Colonies, as Canada was then named, as well as a transcontinental railroad, the development of Canadian literature, and the settling of the West.

A great orator, McGee was elected to the Canadian Legislative Assembly in 1858. He served in positions of leadership until his assassination in 1868. This statue of McGee (opposite page) stands in Montreal.

but they worked nearly one-third of the jobs held by plumbers, steamfitters, and boilermakers. The women mainly were found working in domestic service, in laundries, and in the textile industry.

Irishmen also found success in politics, becoming mayors and senators in the United States and members of Canada's Parliament.

During the 19th and 20th centuries, many Irish Americans became involved in politics. Al Smith became the first Irish American to run for president in 1928; he lost the election to Herbert Hoover. During his political career, Smith also served as governor of New York.

The latter was the case for Thomas D'Arcy McGee, who is known as a "Father of the Canadian Confederation."

Much of the transportation system of the early United States and Canada became a reality because of the hard work of Irish immigrants. Along with working on railroad lines and canals, they were instrumental in building the streetcar systems and roadways.

They also fought in their countries' wars. Many Irish were drafted into the army during the Civil War. More than 144,000

Irish-born troops were part of the Union Army. Irish Americans also served in their country's armed forces during both World War I and World War II. The latter war helped pave the way for many veterans of all backgrounds, including Irish, to further their education once the war was over.

Even though the majority of immigrants came to the New World with few skills, others became prominent lawyers, journalists, archbishops, and businessmen. As time went on, discrimination against those with an Irish heritage also lessened. Proof of that again was seen when John F. Kennedy, the grandson of Irish immigrants, was elected president of the United States in 1960. Other presidents had been able to claim an Irish heritage, but Kennedy was the first Irish American Roman Catholic ever elected president. ✹

6 The Irish Today

Irish immigration changed the face of many communities in Canada and the United States. Imagine, for example, the situation in Boston in 1847. Around 37,000 Irish immigrants had come to that city, accounting for about a third of its population. By 1850, 26 percent of the people living in New York were of Irish descent. Today, more than 40 million Americans can claim Irish blood.

A young girl dressed in traditional Irish knit garb waves an Irish flag during a parade in Chicago. Today, Americans of Irish descent are the third-largest population sub-group in the United States.

The issues for the Irish looking to emigrate to the United States today are different from those experienced in the past. Illegal immigration is a problem found in the United States today. It's estimated that as many as 150,000 illegal Irish immigrants live in the area between Boston and Philadelphia. Many are there for economic reasons, but are unable to enter the country legally because of restrictive immigration laws. The laws include a family preference system in which Irish with siblings or parents living in the United States are admitted to the country relatively easily. This excludes many, but some make their home in the U.S. anyway, easily assimilating into the cities in the Northeast.

AN AMERICAN HERO

When John Fitzgerald Kennedy was sworn in as the 35th president of the United States in 1961, he was the youngest man ever elected to that high office. He was just 43 years old. Also the first Roman Catholic chosen for the post, Kennedy traced his roots back to Ireland. His parents, Joseph Patrick Kennedy and Rose Fitzgerald Kennedy, both had been born in Boston, but his grandparents had been Irish immigrants.

While one might imagine a person who would become president would have a clear vision for his future, Kennedy didn't always know what he wanted to do with his life.

After graduating with honors from Harvard in 1940, he volunteered for service in the army. A weak back prevented him from following this path. But in 1941, after working to strengthen his muscles, Kennedy was accepted into the navy, serving until 1945. As captain of a patrol boat, Kennedy gained national attention as a hero when he saved the members of his crew after the ship was destroyed in the Pacific Ocean.

Before finding his place in politics, Kennedy spent several months working as a newspaper reporter. He would later win the Pulitzer Prize for his book *Profiles in Courage*. The book became a bestseller and made his name a household word.

People who remember Kennedy generally think of him as being healthy and youthful, but appearances can be misleading. He had a bad back after his navy service, and suffered from Addison's disease, which left him weak and caused him to lose weight. He took medication every day to combat the disease.

Kennedy was elected to Congress at age 29, and later became a
senator. After he was elected president, Kennedy worked to ease
suffering both in the United States and abroad. He supported the
civil rights movement, promoted the space program, and launched
the Peace Corps, which sent thousands of Americans overseas to
help developing nations raise their standards of living.

Kennedy's time as president was cut short by an assassin's bullet.
He died in Dallas, Texas, on November 22, 1963.

To help provide day-to-day assistance to recent Irish immigrants, the Emerald Isle Immigration Center (EIIC) was established in 1988. The EIIC has helped thousands of immigrants apply to live in the United States legally. It also offers job training, helps immigrants find work, and focuses on citizenship and voter registration. Those immigrating during the Great Famine undoubtedly would have greatly appreciated such help in their days.

But the past is not forgotten.

Irish Americans and Irish Canadians remain proud of their past as they continue to look toward their future. Irish celebrations are held throughout both countries, and many folks with Irish heritage travel to

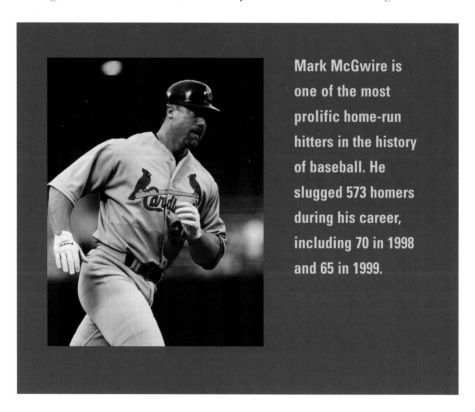

Mark McGwire is one of the most prolific home-run hitters in the history of baseball. He slugged 573 homers during his career, including 70 in 1998 and 65 in 1999.

Frank McCourt won a Pulitzer Prize in 1998 for *Angela's Ashes,* his account of growing up in Ireland and America.

Ireland each year to get a glimpse of "where they came from." Irish culture—from music to movies to old-fashioned storytelling—isn't hard to find, especially on the East Coast.

In Boston, statues of famous Irish Americans—and statues created and designed by Irish-Americans—abound. In fact, a $1 million memorial park was unveiled in Boston in 1998 to commemorate the 150th anniversary of the Irish famine. The Famine Memorial is found along the city's famous Freedom Trail and serves as a reminder to all of what the Irish and other immigrants seek when they brave oceans to come to a new world.

Famous People of Irish Descent

ADVENTURERS

Nellie Bly, journalist and adventuress who traveled around the world in 72 days

Brendan the Navigator, a religious missionary and explorer who, according to Irish myth, proved the existence of land west across the Atlantic Ocean by his voyage in the seventh century

SPORTS

Jimmy Connors, one of the top professional tennis players in the world in the 1970s and 1980s

John McEnroe, who dominated the men's professional tennis tour in the early 1980s

Mark McGwire, record-setting home-run hitter

John L. Sullivan, bare-knuckle boxing champion in the 1880s

ENTERTAINMENT

Mary Higgins Clark, author of many best-selling books, mainly thrillers

Bing Crosby, popular singer and Academy Award-winning actor

F. Scott Fitzgerald, novelist and short-story writer whose books include *The Great Gatsby*

Jackie Gleason, actor and entertainer

Frank McCourt, Pulitzer Prize winning author of *Angela's Ashes*

Edward R. Murrow, one of the most influential journalists in the 20th century

Eugene O'Neill, winner of four Pulitzer Prizes for drama as well as a Nobel Prize for literature

Ed Sullivan, journalist and TV producer, host of *The Ed Sullivan Show*

POLITICS

Richard J. Daley, mayor of Chicago from 1955 until his death in 1976

John F. Kennedy, former president

Sandra Day O'Connor, first woman chosen to serve on the United State Supreme Court

OTHERS

William Bonney, became known as the famous outlaw Billy the Kid

Molly Brown, gained fame by surviving the sinking of the ocean liner *Titanic* in 1912 and was called the "unsinkable Molly Brown"

Henry Ford, pioneering automobile manufacturer who first used the concept of mass production

Margaret Sanger, outspoken advocate for birth control

Annie Sullivan, dubbed "the miracle worker" for her success as the teacher who helped Helen Keller communicate with the world

Blight a disease that causes plants to wither or decay.

Cholera a disease of the stomach and intestines.

Discrimination treating someone badly because they are a different race, religion, or sex.

Emigrate to leave one's country and move to another.

Fertilizer a substance put on land to make it produce more and healthier crops.

Ghetto a part of town where the poor live.

Immune having a high degree of resistance to a disease.

Missionary Someone who works to advance some cause or idea, usually with regards to religious beliefs.

Provision a supply of food and drinks.

Quarantine keeping someone away from others for a time to prevent the spread of contagious diseases.

Ration a food allowance for one day.

Typhus a contagious disease caused by germs carried by fleas and lice.

Further Reading

DeGregorio, William A. *The Complete Book of U.S. Presidents*. New York: Dembner Books, 1989.

Gourley, Catherine. *Wheels of Time: A Biography of Henry Ford*. Brookfield: The Millbrook Press, 1997.

Hoobler, Dorothy, and Thomas Hoobler. *The Irish American Family Album*. New York: Oxford University Press, 1995.

Keneally, Thomas. *The Great Shame*. New York: Anchor Books, 2000.

Laxton, Edward. *The Famine Ships: The Irish Exodus to America*. New York: Henry Holt and Company, 1997.

Levine, L.E. *Young Man in the White House: John Fitzgerald Kennedy*. New York: Julian Messner, Inc., 1964.

Miller, Kerby, and Paul Wagner. *Out of Ireland: The Story of Irish Emigration to America*. Washington, D.C.: Elliott & Clark Publishing, 1994.

Padden, Michael, and Robert Sullivan. *May the Road Rise to Meet You: Everything You Need to Know About Irish American History*. New York: Penguin Group, 1999.

Swisher, Clarice. *John F. Kennedy*. San Diego: Greenhaven Press, Inc., 2000.

Finding Your Irish American Ancestors

Betit, Kyle J., and Dwight A. Radford. *Ireland: A Genealogical Guide*. Salt Lake City: The Irish At Home and Abroad, 1998.

Carmack, Sharon DeBartolo. *A Genealogist's Guide to Discovering Your Immigrant and Ethnic Ancestors*. Cincinnati: Betterway Books, 2000.

Grenham, John. *Tracing Your Irish Ancestors*. Dublin: Gill and Macmillan, 1999.

Hackett, J. Dominick, and Charles M. Early. *Passenger Lists from Ireland*. Baltimore: Clearfield Co., 1994.

Internet Resources

http://www.census.gov

The official website of the U.S. Bureau of the Census contains information about the most recent census taken in 2000.

http://www.statcan.ca/start.html

The website for Canada's Bureau of Statistics, which includes population information updated for the most recent census in July 2001.

http://www.pbs.org/wgbh/pages/irish/

This site contains detailed information on the history of the Irish in America.

http://www.aihs.org

The American Irish Historical Society Web site is aimed at documenting the entire history of the Irish in America and clearing up misconceptions or misrepresentations of fact.

http://www.canadasirishfest.com

Information on Canada's Irish Festival, including presentations, music, speakers, and more.

Index

Photo Credits

Contributors

Barry Moreno has been librarian and historian at the Ellis Island Immigration Museum and the Statue of Liberty National Monument since 1988. He is the author of *The Statue of Liberty Encyclopedia*, which was published by Simon & Schuster in October 2000. He is a native of Los Angeles, California. After graduation from California State University at Los Angeles, where he earned a degree in history, he joined the National Park Service as a seasonal park ranger at the Statue of Liberty; he eventually became the monument's librarian. In his spare time, Barry enjoys reading, writing, and studying foreign languages and grammar. His biography has been included in *Who's Who Among Hispanic Americans*, *The Directory of National Park Service Historians*, *Who's Who in America*, and *The Directory of American Scholars*.

Brenda Haugen, a graduate of the University of North Dakota in Grand Forks, is an award-winning journalist and freelance editor. She lives in Jordan, Minnesota.